Victory…
Your Only Option

Freida McCullough

Copyright © 2021 Freida McCullough

ISBN: 9798705319190

DEDICATION

I dedicate this book to my mother Mary Elizabeth Richardson. She was my mom, my encourager, and my friend. She was loved by so many because of her generous heart and infectious spirit. Her smile and gorgeous hazel eyes would light up a room. She was a beautiful woman

who commanded attention without saying a word when she walked into any place.

My mother was a brave woman. She overcame many challenges in her life and accomplished amazing things despite many obstacles. She was a teenage mom who raised four beautiful daughters to be strong, respectful, and accomplished women. She required excellence and she served with excellence.

Mom was a devoted wife of forty-seven years. She was the grandmother of five grandchildren and a great grandmother to her only great-granddaughter, all of whom she absolutely loved. She was a true servant that loved God with all her heart. Not only did she love God, but she also loved God's people.

Mom left us sooner than we wanted, but she left an

indelible impact on all of us. It is because of her love and support that I am able to write this book. Although she knew I was writing this book, she never got a chance to read it. I pray that it makes her proud.

I will forever cherish her for all she taught me and all she sacrificed for our family. She will forever be my hero. I love you, Momma!

Table of Contents

ACKNOWLEDGMENTS

First, to my amazing husband...
for his love and support. Thank you honey for always
being there and pushing me to THRIVE! You are the love
of my life, and I will love you forever.

To my children Eryn and Shane...
You are the best part of me, and I am thankful that God
allowed me to be your mother. I love you with all my
heart.

*To my newest joy, my granddaughter
Oaklynn Reign...*
You have brought me so much joy at a time of sorrow.
God knew your presence was needed in my life and I am
overjoyed to be your Mimi.

To my wonderful father Mitchell Richardson...
Thank you for all your encouraging words and for always
instilling in me that no matter what room I walked into, I
deserved to be there just as much as the next person. I am
confident because of you. I love you, daddy.

To my sisters Stephanie, Tanisha and Keleni...
Thank you for loving me for who I am. I am honored to
call you my friends as well as sisters.

ACKNOWLEDGMENTS (CONT.)

Finally, to my team: Thank you!
Daphne, Dagne and Lakesha…

Cover Design
Daphne Register
iDAP Marketing
www.idapmarketing.com

Lakesha McDonald
Creatively For You Designs
www.creativelyforyou.com

Book Editor
Dagne Barton
ValUAdded Coaching & Consulting
www.DagneBarton.com

Photographer
Daphne Register
iDAP Marketing
www.idapmarketing.com

INTRODUCTION

Sometimes, life can be so challenging that given the option, you would choose to quit. You would not necessarily stop living, but just give up on what is causing you difficulty. In all actuality, many people have resigned from life. They have just completely given up. I want to tell you that even though it may be hard, seem hopeless, and your options appear limited, be hopeful because when you are in Christ, **VICTORY IS YOUR ONLY OPTION**. Jesus tells us in John 16:33 that we do not have to worry because he has already overcome the world.

> *"I have told you these things, so that in me you may have peace. In this world, you will have trouble. But take heart! I have overcome the world."*

In other words, He has already secured victory for us. I understand that as you read this, you think, "but you do not know my situation. You have no idea what I am going through. You don't know how hard it is to hang in there." You are right. I don't know anything about your specific situation, but I do know the same God who did it for me will be able to do the same for you. I don't want to trivialize anything you are going through. I simply want to help you change your perspective about what you are going through or may experience in the future.

If you don't have the option to quit... you won't quit. If winning is your only choice, then, of course, you will choose to win. How do I know this? Because no one wants to lose. I don't believe anyone ever sets out to be defeated. It's just that life can sometimes make you want to throw in the towel and surrender to your circumstances, instead of being determined to succeed in every situation.

In my life, there were plenty of times when I found myself at crossroads. At those times, I asked myself, do I give up now, or do I keep going until I walk into my victory? The truth is, at times I weighed the options and thought quitting might be easier than continuing to fight. I didn't want to muster up the strength to persevere and of course, the enemy gave me all kinds of options, none of which included VICTORY. His options were never meant to be any good for me.

I don't want you to think that I always made the right choice because I didn't. There were times I fell for the tricks of the enemy and decided I didn't want to be victorious. I believed resigning myself to defeat was much easier. As crazy as that may sound, it was a reality I had to deal with. There were times when defeat was just the easy option. Sometimes I just didn't have the strength to fight. However, I would remind myself that though it was easier to quit, if you stop, you will never see what you have been fighting for.

Writing this book posed a challenge and I had to decide. Was I going to be defeated and stop writing because I felt a block, lost inspiration, or faced challenges, or would I push through to the end and obtain my victory? Well, the very fact that you are reading this book makes it obvious that I took the choice of defeat off the table, making victory my only option. Although I didn't meet my first, second, third, or fourth deadline, I didn't give up, although I really wanted to. It was challenging and I stopped and started many times, but I pressed on to the end. No matter how hard it was or how long it took, I only had one option— and that was to WIN! I had to keep pushing until I finished.

Is that you right now? I believe what I went through in my life was to help you with where you are right now. I want to help you clear the table of all the other options, so you can walk to your victory. I want you to soar and experience everything God has in store for you! My heart wants to see you walk into and live a life of success and prosperity. Even on days that are not the best, you can still be triumphant because situations and circumstances do not void your victory. I want you to know that no matter what you are facing, you can overcome it! You can achieve success!

I pray that by the time you finish this book, you would have received a shot of strength and courage that will make you walk with your head up. I want you to gain a fresh wind and change your posture of defeat to that of the winner you are! I want you to straighten your slumped shoulders and lift your chin. Take your place because you have so much awaiting you. Stop sitting on the sidelines and get into the game, because your victory is beckoning to you! V's up...let's go!

V's UP

VICTORY TRAINING

I have not served in the military. However, my father and my husband are both Air Force veterans. My father served for twenty-four years, and my husband for twenty years and twenty days, as he loves to say. One thing I observed about both my father and my husband is when they were on active duty, they were constantly training. Although nothing was going on and the country was not at war, they had training exercises, during which they would prepare for war in case they ever had to go to battle. They spent time rehearsing the mission and sharpening their processes. Their military unit planned for what could happen.

Although my dad was an aircraft scheduler and my husband a security police officer, they both had to participate in the base-wide training exercises. No matter what their job, they were required to train.

It is the same when it comes to achieving victory in your life. You cannot wait until there is a crisis to start training. Training is an ongoing activity. What do I mean by training? I mean, if you want to have a victorious life, you must constantly prepare. In other words, you must be consistent in reading your Bible and praying. You must be a person of worship, and praise must be a staple in your everyday life. You cannot expect to know how to use your weapons if you wait until you are in the middle of the battle to pick them up and learn how to use them. If you do not know what to read, purchase a devotional or download a devotional app on your phone. Finding a way to connect to God is made easier partly because of technology and the access we have to the internet.

You cannot be proficient in something until you take the time to understand how to use it. I know this can sound like a cliché, but I can tell you from personal experience—it works! I have tried it myself and I have also tried living without it. Often, we discount the simple things because we are looking for something grand and powerful when all we need is a little practice on the weapons we already have.

What are those weapons? I am glad you asked! Some of the basic weapons include prayer, the word of God, praise, worship, speaking life, and speaking the word. These are not new, and to some, may even seem outdated. I promise you, none of these weapons will ever be obsolete. They will always be effective in obtaining and sustaining victory, in the life of every believer. So often, we desire to work with deep things when we have not mastered the basics. Stop reading right here and say this out aloud…"It is a process!"

You are not expected to know how to use everything, but you should learn and expand your proficiency in using any of the weapons through training.

There are other weapons such as praying in the Spirit, and the power that comes with being baptized in the Holy Spirit. I don't want to label them as advanced, but I will say it takes walking with God with the basics before you are often able to utilize these weapons effectively.

Another part of your training is learning to stop doubting
*Mark 11: 22-23 reads: "Then Jesus said to the disciples,
"Have faith in God. 23 I tell you the truth, you can say to
this mountain, 'May you be lifted up and thrown into the
sea,' and it will happen. But you must believe it will
happen and have no doubt in your heart."*
Don't just go through the motions in prayer but believe
with your heart and soul when you pray. God has proven
Himself and will continue to do so, as you learn to trust
Him more.

I am not saying that there will never be a time when you
question where you are or even have moments of doubt,
but you cannot stay in that place. Scripture tells us that
you *will* have those moments of doubt or unbelief. When
you do, all you have to do is to tell Him, '*Lord, I believe but
help my unbelief.*' This is saying that even though I trust,
doubt creeps in now and then. Believe me, I have certainly
experienced this. I understand what it's like to know the
Word and doubt the Word at the same time. My faith has
been shaken to the core. I had to sit back and evaluate
what I honestly believed. I know you are reading this and
saying, "how is that possible, you are a "woman of God." I
don't want to label myself as such, but I will say I am a
believer and just like other believers, life's challenges can
shake the very core of who you are and what you believe. I
will discuss this more in the upcoming chapters.

The key is to strengthen your faith to the point that your
doubt is not as strong as your faith. I passionately believe
that you can get to a point where you rarely go through
stages of uncertainty, if at all.

You must stretch and strengthen your faith if you are going to walk in victory. Winners undergo strength training as part of their everyday workout routine. They understand that strength is a basic requirement of a champion. The same is true of your faith. It must be increased as a part of your basic walk if you plan to be successful at whatever you go through. As the core of the body is the center of balance and strength in your natural body, faith is the same for the spirit.

Additionally, part of training is being focused and purposeful. For instance, the number of reps and the combination of weight make a difference in how you build your muscles. You work legs one day, back another, shoulders after that, then chest and last, the arms. This is to ensure you cover every part of the body. If you expect to achieve results, you must be intentional and not just go through the motions like a person who goes to the gym just to check a box but has no real expectation of results.

To avoid fatigue, try not to focus on how long you have been going through the situation. Don't concentrate on your circumstances. In the old church, they would use the word 'weary.' Once you get tired/weary, your expectation begins to erode, and when you have no expectation, it becomes easier to start looking for options other than victory. You will do anything for relief and that is a bad position to be in.

One of the things I do when I run on the treadmill at the gym is cover the time, so I do not focus on how long I have been running. I simply put on my headset and play something on my phone such as a tv show I want to catch up on. When I do this, I can run effortlessly because my attention is not on how long I have been running. I can stay on because I have an expectation of getting to the end of the episode I started. Now I have a purpose for the time it takes to finish the workout.

You must have an "I want to see my victory" mindset when dealing with your situation. The great thing for believers is that we already know we will win if only we can just endure if we simply hold on...

> Isaiah 40:31 says, *"We will mount up on wings as an eagle, we will run and not be weary and we will walk and will not faint."*

We don't prevail when we don't train. Honey...training is not easy, but it is *necessary*. The world understands the importance of training; therefore, we as believers need to understand that we must also train to emerge triumphantly.

Training is just preparation. The presence of the Holy Spirit does not mean a lack of training. I think we take the scriptural text that I can do all things through Christ a little too literally. Yes, the Holy Spirit is there as our guide, but we are still expected to play a part in our own victory, and our part is to prepare. We must put in the work. In John Chapter 9, Jesus heals a blind man. In this text, He takes clay, puts it on the man's eyes, and tells him to go wash in the pool. I believe that Jesus could have healed the man without adding the extra step of his having to go wash in the pool, but He wanted the man to participate in his miracle. The man did not have to perform the miracle, but he did have a part to play, however minor. He had to put in the work, and if you want to walk in your victory, you too will have to put in the work. You must participate in your miracle.

When I go to the gym with my husband, one thing I do not like is strength training. I do not like having to go to the gym, and there are times that I whine and complain about training more than others. The lazy part of me wants to find other ways to get the same results without having to go through the process of training. I want to be able to lie in the bed and burn calories as I sleep. I think that rolling over in the bed should count as a form of cardio to assist in weight loss! I know that is not how it works, but a girl can dream!

Back to my gym analogy. I gave my husband a hard time, constantly pouting and trying to talk my way out of doing those squats or lifting weights. I would rather sit on the machines and work at my own pace, which is slow and light. I had to realize that if I wanted real results, I had to be challenged. I had to tackle the hard things. I had to push myself even when I didn't want to, and I had to keep going even when I wanted to stop.

Here is a tip: Stop asking God to give you real results

when you don't want to put in the effort to push yourself. This may sound a little hard but the results you get are direct reflections of the effort you do or do not put in.

I say this to motivate you to push yourself. Push even when you are tired. Push even when you are disappointed. Push even when you are discouraged. Push even when you don't feel like you have it all together! Push for your victory!

I want you to try something different. I want you to change the way you have been engaging in your spiritual preparation. I promise when you change your perspective, focus on your success and not the situation, and become more intentional, you will see different results.

Victory Notes

Thought Prompters:
In what areas do I need more training?
How can I push myself more? What situation have I been
so focused on that I could not see my victory?

_____

_____

_____

_____

_____

_____

_____

_____

_____

_____

_____

_____

_____

_____

_____

_____

_____

THE BATTLE

We just finished talking about training. This preparation is not just to have something to do. We want victory but what you have to understand is it presupposes a battle. You cannot get the victory if there is no fight or enemy. Victory means overcoming a struggle or an enemy. The Bible says no weapon formed against you shall prosper. (*Isaiah 54:17*). This means that the weapon *will* form. In other words, the enemy *will* come against you. Life *will* come against you, but it doesn't mean you don't have victory. Obstacles will come, but never let an obstacle make you stop or take a defeated position. You may have to press pause, but you can always start again…JUST DON'T STOP!

The good news is that barriers can be removed. So often, the devil tries to make you believe that you do not have victory because you are having problems. I think everyone can raise their hand in agreement that they have had to overcome a struggle, or an enemy, at one time in their life. We all have, including me. I have personally struggled in my marriage, my business, and ministry. I am bold enough to declare that most of us have some battle scars that remind us of what we have been through.

Let's return to my analogy of the gym. One day, I was working out on the elliptical, and I looked down at the stickers on the front. I noticed one of them said there were eight levels of resistance to allow you to progress over time. The Holy Spirit whispered quietly, "That is the same in the spirit". I quickly understood that with every level, there will be another degree of resistance. We often get excited when we receive a prophetic word about moving to a higher level. If you are like me, you have great ideas about a business or project and you are motivated to get started. However, we must realize that going to the next stage means the resistance will increase. The saying is, "new level, new devil," which is just another way of saying the devil is not going to allow you to just walk into what God has for you. The devil is like the defense on a football team doing everything he can to stop you from getting to the end zone. He is going to block, tackle, and run you down, to stop you from scoring in life. But unlike football, in life, you get more than four quarters to win. Plus, you have the best coach if you would just listen to the plays He sends on the field.

Half the battle of winning is understanding there will be a battle. So often, people give up on their dreams and plans because they face resistance. They assume it means they are not supposed to move forward. Most of the time, it is quite the opposite. The resistance is just an indication you have just shifted to another point. Don't run from the opposition. Learn how to adjust your breathing and your stride to withstand the challenge you now encounter.

What does that look like? It means you now find yourself shifting your concentration to prayer and devotion time. Your worship time becomes more intense and frequent. Sometimes, you must slow down and take longer strides when you feel resistance, and you certainly must focus. If you don't concentrate on getting to the end and change your mindset from thinking about the challenge to thinking about finishing, you will quit. You will give up. I have seen this happen to people many a time. They hit a rough spot or make a mistake, and the pressure of trying to be "perfect" or the thought of what others say about them causes them to retreat. The devil makes them feel they cannot recover. The struggle becomes too great, they only focus on what went wrong (the battle) and they give up.

Your attention is the key. Sometimes, the resistance can get very hard; your body goes into the protection mode and begins to signal to your mind to quit. That is why the Bible says we walk by faith and not by sight because, given the opportunity to give up, we will. You cannot let your body dictate your progress. You must keep your mind on the finish line.

Let me encourage you! No matter what you have done... no matter what mistakes or so-called "failures" have occurred in your life...know that God is with you. There is nothing you can do to make Him walk away from you.

> *Deuteronomy 31:8 The Lord himself goes before you and will be with you; he will never leave you nor forsake you. Do not be afraid; do not be discouraged."*

So often we look at people's negative responses to our issues and think that is how God looks at us. Thank goodness that is not how He sees us! Winning the battle will require that you see Him for who He is and how He sees you. You must focus on who God made you to be and what He created you to do. You must concentrate on the fact that He has a plan for your life.

Another way to stay engaged when you are dealing with a struggle or a battle is to learn to concentrate on something or somebody else, instead of focusing all your attention on what you are going through. Focus on serving someone else or something else. In other words, don't magnify your situation, but magnify God in the situation. Make God and doing His will the priority. He will strengthen you so you can endure. You will also find joy and a sense of accomplishment when focused on helping others.

This is not always easy to do. Of course, you want to devote all your thoughts and energy to handle what is going on in your world! But turning your attention to serving others centers your thoughts on the reality that you are not the only one dealing with issues. Often, you will discover most of the time that someone else has a bigger battle than you. This does not mean you are comparing, but it puts things in perspective.

Battles will come. Sometimes you find yourself fighting multiple conflicts. Believe me, I have been in a place when it seems you cannot catch a break. It is one thing after another. Dealing with battles can be physically, emotionally, and mentally exhausting. It can affect your health, and you may not even realize why your body is responding the way it is. It is important to schedule regular checkups with your doctor, especially during times of crisis or when dealing with difficult times in your life. Getting therapy or counseling is not only important but also most definitely ok. You must find time to rest and clear your mind so that you can mentally and physically handle the challenge.

Therefore, having previously trained yourself in prayer and reading your Word is vital. Your attention must shift from the resistance you are facing to the Word.

The Bible says, "*The race is not given to the swift nor the strong, but to the one that endures until the end*" Eccl. 9:11

It is at these times that songs begin to flow out of your heart to encourage you. Portions from a sermon you heard will rise in your spirit; things you have read in your time of devotion or "training times," will help you find your second wind. You will find yourself in a position to push.

Yes, you are in the battle, but be encouraged to keep going because now you have victory in your sight.

Victory Notes

Thought Prompters:
Acknowledge my battles.
How do my battles make me feel?
How do I approach my battles?

_____

_____

_____

_____

_____

_____

_____

_____

_____

_____

_____

_____

_____

_____

_____

_____

_____

PERSONAL BATTLES

Sometimes people look at you from the outside and think you have never been through anything. I believe that is both positive and negative. I may not reflect what I have been through, but I have been through some struggles. I have had to fight some enemies. Although it is good that we may not bear evidence of what we have been through, sometimes people who are in the middle of something may not take your advice to heart, under the impression that you can't relate. After all, your battle scars are not on display. I am not saying you should walk around exposing everything, but please know that just because you can't see my scars, it doesn't mean I haven't been in a battle. The great part is, I have been through some fights, and I came out victorious! If you will allow me, let's journey through a few struggles I have been through and a few enemies I have had to face in my life. I pray that my testimony will encourage you, should you find yourself in a struggle.

CHILDHOOD

There is no other way to start the next sentence gently, so let me just start here. I was molested by my babysitter's son at the age of four. I never told my mother and father because I really didn't understand what was going on at the time. It wasn't until I was an adult that I even remembered that it even happened. I believe I just suppressed it. I had flashbacks of it but couldn't for the life of me figure out what I was seeing. I couldn't grasp whether it was something that really happened, or something I saw in a movie that I was putting myself in. I didn't even connect it to my low self-esteem issues. I didn't connect it to my closing myself off to my own husband. I just tucked it away, but it still created struggles in my life. The enemy wanted to make me self-destruct by creating a conflict in my mind.

Often, people struggle so much with situations in their minds, that they end up fighting internally more than they do externally. The battle that is waged in the mind is dangerous if you do not learn to be open and talk to someone. You are fighting yourself and that is a dangerous thing to do. Let me stop and tell you that it is ok to seek godly help and counsel. Let's dispel the stigma of seeking external help to be able to process what we go through.

I grew up in times when going to a therapist was not in tune with faith. In other words, it was a "ding" against your faith. You were made to feel you didn't trust God because you sought help from man. Thank goodness I know better now. I now understand that good, godly, professional counsel, along with prayer and fasting, are just as effective. They all work together.

Let's fast forward a few years to middle school and high school when I dealt with my self-image and self-worth. It is not that I was not getting affirmation at home. I think a lot of it was nothing more than growing up and being an adolescent. My father and mother both lavished attention on me and my sisters and constantly taught us life lessons.

I just had an internal struggle, as so many do.

I know I am not alone. You are reading this book and you are still engaged in an internal struggle with your self-image and self-worth. You are like the eight spies that came back to give Moses the report on the Promised Land. You see yourself as a grasshopper in your own eyes. You see what you could be, but you allow your thoughts and perspectives about yourself to make you walk away from what you see. You see into your future, yet settle for your present and allow your past to arrest you. Can I give you some advice? You cannot access your future holding on to your past and settling for your present. You must learn to fight the conflict of your mind and your past. For some, it is not just the struggle of what you think of yourself, but the conflict of fighting what others say about you, or what others have done to you. Often, we allow the world and people's perceptions and expectations to push us into battles.

In high school, I struggled with my appearance. I was very skinny and didn't have the shape the more "popular" girls had. I am sure many of you can relate... My parents were a part of the holiness church and very conservative, so I grew up not wearing pants. This also made me look different and children can be cruel. I was picked on for being the "church girl" and, although I had some good friends that loved me despite the way I dressed, I still felt like I was so different...and
truth to tell, I was. I just didn't realize at the time that I was different because I was me. I didn't know who I was, so I couldn't love ME!

Let me encourage you! Don't be discouraged if you don't

"fit the mold". You were born to stand out! I hope you hear what I am telling you. Close your eyes and let this sink in. So often, we are told that we must look a certain way, act a certain way, and dress a certain way. We are given "the rules" and if we do not follow them, we are treated as if something is wrong with us. But be ok with being yourself! Learn to "be free to be me". Love the "me' in yourself! When we learn to love ourselves, we can properly love others.

That skinny young lady grew up and she discovered her confidence. She had challenges and still faces opposition, but she is still walking in her stride! Every day and every year, she is growing and developing and blossoming into what God wants her to be. Yes, I am talking about myself! You need to encourage yourself. It is often easier for us to encourage others and show others grace, more than we do ourselves. Sometimes you must look at yourself like you are someone else. In other words, look at yourself from the outside. Change your perspective of who you are!

Victory Notes

Thought Prompters:
How do I see myself?

_____

_____

_____

_____

_____

_____

_____

_____

_____

_____

_____

_____

_____

_____

_____

_____

_____

_____

BECOMING A WOMAN

I graduated high school and got caught up in a couple of relationships that were not good for me. One guy only wanted sex and, again, because I didn't know who I was, I gave myself to someone who wasn't worthy of me. I even found myself in a very brief relationship with someone who, I later discovered through a very good friend, was married. I immediately broke that relationship off because regardless of my insecurities, that was one line I was not willing to cross.

These two relationships happened between the ages of eighteen and nineteen. When I was nineteen, I moved to Germany with my family. I gave my life to the Lord, started serving in the church, and was sold out for the Lord. I was only focused on my Lord and Savior Jesus Christ. It was quite a turn from the last paragraph (LOL). Then I met a young man in the chapel, and we began to date. Everyone thought we were the "perfect" couple and so did I. After dating for about eight months, he came to me one day to let me know that he no longer wanted to be in a relationship with me. There was another young woman in the chapel that he wanted to be with. I was hurt, angry, and embarrassed, and it was another blow to my self-esteem because I thought there was something wrong with me. I felt like someone had punched me in the stomach! I was sick. On top of all those emotions I was dealing with, I had to watch passively as they dated and developed a relationship right before me. Being overseas, I could not just run to another church to avoid seeing them.

As we didn't have a lot to choose from, if I wanted to go to church, I had to go there. I must admit, it was a painful process, and there were many times I just wanted to run, cry or just hide, but I stayed. I stayed and watched them get married. She even invited me to her bridal shower. CRAZY, I KNOW RIGHT? Now, I am not going to pretend like I was just ok with it at that point...nope, I was not. I did not attend. I didn't love Jesus that much yet LOL!

I recall telling God I was hurting and lonely and I remember Him telling me, "I hear you. You may be hurting right now but you are not alone." About a month later, I met the man that would be my husband. God already knew he had Mack McCullough on reserve for me. He knew what was best for me.

Here is the thing: I met Mack in the chapel—the same place where I felt my pain, the same place I felt my embarrassment, the same place I wanted to run from. Had I not stayed, I would not have met him. I stayed and I did not quit. In the end, I got VICTORY! We have been married since July 1992. Yes, we have had some battles (that is another book), but even amidst that, we continue to declare that for our marriage, Victory is...Our Only Option.

Let me encourage you! Your victory will be found right where you are...in the middle of your pain, embarrassment, and frustration. Don't run, stay put! God is preparing the table for you. You won't be able to enjoy the sweet taste of victory from the meal God has prepared for you if you leave too soon.

Victory Notes

Thought Prompters:
What battles have you encountered as you grew that
challenged you but made you better?

_____

_____

_____

_____

_____

_____

_____

_____

_____

_____

_____

_____

_____

_____

_____

_____

_____

W AS A DAUGHTER

While writing this book, I had to face several battles. One was that my mother was diagnosed with lung cancer in May 2019. That was a blow to my family. My mother was not, and never had been, a smoker. She appeared to be perfectly healthy, vibrant, and active. I remember hearing those words about her illness and all I could do was just sit there. My family had to process this situation and we didn't even know how to do it. It was hard to believe it was happening. She didn't just say what I think she said??

We began to go to her appointments with her, and the doctor talked about treatment. He said they would do surgery to remove the lower section of the affected lung and things looked good. They did scans and said the cancer had not spread, so removing the section of the lung should work. They told us she would not need chemo or radiation.

We were prayerful and looking at the future with cautious optimism. The day of her surgery dawned, and we all gathered around the bed and prayed. We were believing God for healing and successful surgery. They told us the procedure would take five to six hours. They rolled her back and we sat in the waiting room. About two hours into the surgery, the nurse came out and said they were closing her up and the doctor wanted to see us. As we entered the consultation room, the doctor came in right behind us. He informed us that when they went in, they found some of the lymph nodes around the lung looking infected and after biopsy, discovered the cancer had spread. They did not remove the tumor because they needed to start chemo and radiation immediately. I remember my family sitting there. We were all in a daze, then the tears started flowing. We all retreated into our own space to try to process what the doctor had told us. After an hour, my sisters and I came together in the waiting room. We began to encourage one another to stay strong and we fortified our bond and our resolve to be there for our mother and our father.

I remember as we were sitting there, my youngest sister declared, "We have trusted God all these years, we can't stop trusting Him now." We all agreed that day that we would trust God. In other words, we decided that victory was our only option. My mother had several issues with chemo and radiation, was hospitalized, and even had to have a feeding tube during the process. However, through it all, we continued to speak life and declare that victory was our only option. Even when she couldn't do it for herself, we declared it for her.

I am sad to say that this battle did not end the way we had hoped, prayed, and believed. On July 11, 2020, my mother passed away. We were devastated. Our world had changed forever. I remember we prayed until minutes before she died that God would work a miracle in her natural body, but His answer was no. As Bishop Geoffrey Vincent Dudley, Sr. said at her service, my mom was ready for the "no" but when everything cleared, I wasn't. To be honest, I didn't know how to deal with that. I felt in my spirit that victory was my only option, but my heart was broken. At this time, my heart was aching so much I couldn't even focus on the victory. Now, here I was left to practice all that I had preached to others. All the things I had written in my book about victory being my only option, and I couldn't get it together. My mom was such an important part of my life, and I could not imagine living every day without her. The adjustment is sometimes overwhelming.

It took me over a year to even start writing again and when I did, I had such a bad mental block I found myself distracted and doing other things. Anything to keep me from dealing with the pain. I missed deadline after deadline. I just wanted to give up. But you are reading this book as proof that I **did not**! I know it will get better with time, but the process is painful. I can truly say that I have made it as far as I have because of the training I had before this. There were days that I couldn't pray or worship. All I could do was cry. There were times I didn't want to feel anything because it hurt too much. I will continue to depend on God because I know victory is my only option. My mom would not want me to quit. She would encourage me as she always did to be everything God created me to be.

Therefore, I continue day by day, declaring the victory in my life. Yes, even at this painful time. Yes, even when I can't seem to get it together. Yes, even when I am not feeling like it. I declare Victory Is My Only Option!

Victory Notes

Thought Prompters:

What battles have you faced in your family?
What impact did it have on the way you viewed your victory?

_____

_____

_____

_____

_____

_____

_____

_____

_____

_____

_____

_____

_____

_____

_____

_____

_____

_____

AS A MOTHER

Another challenge presented itself when my twenty-two-year-old, unmarried daughter told me she was pregnant. She was in her senior year of college, and we had plans for what she was going to do after college. I remember when she called me. Well, she told me that Sunday that she had been feeling nauseous and she couldn't figure out what was going on with her stomach. I didn't think anything of it because she had some stomach issues the previous year. She called me on Monday morning to say she still wasn't feeling well and that she had made a doctor's appointment for the next day. When I got up Tuesday morning, the Spirit quietly whispered to me, "She is pregnant". I tried to ignore the voice I heard and continued getting dressed. My daughter called me to ask me something about her insurance, and I asked her whether she was pregnant. She began to cry, and her response was, "I don't know, maybe". My heart sank, but I still would not believe it.

Now, let me preface this story by telling you I had fired an employee the previous Friday, and the replacement was starting that morning. Additionally, my mother who was battling cancer was not doing very well at that time. I had a lot on my plate. Emotionally, I was drained, and I was dealing with a little anxiety that morning.

I went into my office. When I got there, another employee, who had only worked at my company for two weeks, met me at the door. She walked to her office, put down her keys, and told me, "I quit because I am moving" She then proceeded to walk out the door as my new employee was walking in. I felt like the walls were closing around me. I got through the day. My daughter called around 4:45 p.m. to inform me that she was, indeed, pregnant. All I could do was just yell Eryn noooooo! I didn't even have enough tears to shed. I just sat there with my head in my hands. I could not wrap my mind around it. This was just too much. There was a sick feeling in my stomach, and I wanted to throw up. My daughter was hysterical and distraught, but I could not give her anything and I said just that. "I don't have anything for you." I just sat there. My daughter needed me, but at that moment, I didn't have any comfort to offer her.

I had to process this information along with everything else that was going on. It took me two days to talk to her. During those two days, the enemy kept bringing up thoughts of defeat and discouragement. All I could think was, "She is too young. She is not married. She is not ready. She hasn't graduated from college." Yes, I understand that it was a part of me working through the information, but all I could think about was negative. Every thought I had was about what she wasn't instead of what she was and what she could be. The Spirit had to arrest me and speak to me about the situation. Was I going to choose defeat, or was victory going to be the only option for my child? Once I pushed all the thoughts of defeat off the table, the Spirit began to open my eyes to the victory side. He began to show me who she was and what possibilities there were in this situation. I started giving a victorious response to every negative thought I had. So instead of saying, "She is too young," I said, "She is only a year younger than I was when I had her". Instead of, "She is not married," I said, "she is in a committed relationship with the father, and they can still get married" (by the way, they did get married). Instead of saying, "She is not ready," I said, "She has a job and a great support system". Instead of saying, "She hasn't graduated from college," I told myself, "She will graduate before the baby arrives". I had to take everything the enemy was saying to me, turn it around, and declare that victory was her only option. You have to learn to open your mouth and speak of success amidst your battles. When the enemy is throwing darts of unbelief and doubt, open your mouth and combat it with positive affirmations and Bible verses. His tactics cannot succeed against the truth of God's word!

I wasn't looking at what a blessing my grandchild would be because I was focused only on the circumstances surrounding her getting here. Remember, in the earlier chapter, I talked about what you focus on affecting your ability to achieve victory. I was too busy concentrating on all the things that I didn't think lined up that I almost missed the opportunity to enjoy my first grandchild.

Now, my beautiful granddaughter helps to encourage me on days when the pain of missing my mother becomes too intense. I can hold her and see my mom in her, and she just makes me smile. She was six weeks old when my mother passed away. My mother was so excited to spend time with her. I was able to get pictures of my mom (her GiGi) and the baby two days before my mom passed away. We will cherish those memories forever.

The enemy comes to steal, kill, and destroy. That includes stealing the moments that are meant to be enjoyed. What bad situation are you so focused on that you are missing your moments? Don't be so focused on the circumstances that you miss the opportunity to see victory!

Victory Notes

Thought Prompters:
If you are a parent, what battles have you had or are
facing with your child/children?
How do you maintain a victorious position?

_____

_____

_____

_____

_____

_____

_____

_____

_____

_____

_____

_____

_____

_____

_____

_____

 AS A BUSINESS OWNER

My battles have not all been personal. There were some relating to my business as well. I received my license on December 23, 2000, after failing the state test once. Did I mention I also failed my course test the first time? You are given two opportunities to pass, and I passed the second time by just one point!

As I started my business, I worked hard and overcame some challenges, entering the market at an opportune time. From 2001 to 2007, things were going great. I was making more money than I ever had in my life. I was well into a six-figure income. In December 2005, I started my own real estate company with a business partner. Things were going exceptionally well. We had approximately thirty agents. We had purchased acreage on the main highway in town. We were building our new beautiful commercial plaza that would be our new location, as well as retail space for other businesses.

Our business was growing. Everyone knew our story. We were featured in a magazine and had our faces on mobile billboards. Then, in 2008, the market crashed, and the battles now turned into full-blown war. As you know, real estate is a commission-based business, and when sales slow down, so does income. This was not just business income, but personal income. Here we were in the middle of the market crash, moving into this new building. Sales were down. Agents were leaving the business due to a lack of work, which affected the real estate income. My builders were going out of business because of the housing market downturn. By the way, did I mention we had just started the church in January 2007 and moved into our new home in June 2007?

There were times when my personal income was not enough to meet all our financial obligations. In fact, in 2008, I had no income for three months straight. In 2009, we had an $18,000 monthly mortgage on the building, when we moved in. During the recession, I was battling not giving up, trusting God. There were times I woke up in the middle of the night, overwhelmed, and unable to breathe. I had anxiety attacks and yes, there were times I cried. I am telling you this because people look at what you have and think everything is glamorous, but believe me, it is not all glamorous. There was still a battle. There was a battle in my mind and a battle in my spirit. I saw the reality of what was going on. My mind was ready to quit, but my spirit was fighting back. My mind would say, "...you are going to lose it; ...this is going to drive you crazy," but my spirit would kick in with the Word that I already had inside me. I heard,

> Philippians 4:6, "Don't worry about anything; instead, pray about everything." Tell God what you need and thank Him for all he has done."

In a battle, strategy is key and in this particular battle, strategy was critical because I had to depend on the Holy Spirit to help navigate me through all of this. Of course, prayer became a priority, not just to keep me sane, but also so my husband and I could be positioned to hear the Spirit give us strategic orders.

I recall one day after coming out of prayer, when I walked by the basement door, my husband was coming up the stairs from his prayer time. He looked at me and said, "God said we will not lose anything". This was amidst our looking at the bills piling up and the income dwindling fast. I did not know how it would all work out, but what I did know was that VICTORY WAS OUR ONLY OPTION. My trust in God began to grow even more, and I began to listen intently to the Spirit for direction in my business and at home. The Spirit gave me instructions and had me pick up the phone and call particular people to connect with in business. He began to speak to me about increasing the property management side of the business to increase revenue in the business.

I followed His instructions and property management sustained the company until the market bounced back. Eventually, we were able to get back on our feet. My business has taught me to rely on God.

Victory Notes

Thought Prompters:
How can I be successful in my career/business?
What am I trusting God to do in my career/business?

_____

_____

_____

_____

_____

_____

_____

_____

_____

_____

_____

_____

_____

_____

_____

_____

_____

RECOGNIZE YOUR ENEMY

You must assess your battle to determine your strategy. No good commander goes into combat without a solid strategy. A combat plan cannot be determined until you first determine who the enemy is and where they are located. Many a time, we waste time fighting the wrong enemy and get frustrated. We squander energy and time on the wrong things. It is not because we don't have the training and correct tools, but because we fight the wrong enemy. In every war, they gather what is called intel, which is basically information about the enemy and the entire situation. In other words, they look at the big picture. Part of having a successful approach is being able to see the situation from all angles. We often focus solely on what we are going through. How it makes ME feel…what I am going through…How this is affecting ME! We lose sight of everything and everyone connected to us who are also affected if we do not use wisdom and execute a well-planned and well-advised strategy.

When researching military strategies, you will find many of them having concepts in common. One type is offensive. An offensive tactic is actively going after the enemy. This means studying your enemies' moves to determine their routines and tactics and going after them preemptively before they strike. In the Spirit, this type of strategy looks like praying daily, not just when something happens. Preemptive prayer is having a relationship and staying in a posture of prayer with God. This way, He speaks to you regularly, giving you direction in life and revelation about the Word that will help prevent unfavorable things in your life. There is a saying that if you stay ready, you won't have to get ready. Offensive prayer is like that. You find yourself always praying and therefore always prepared.

When you pray offensively, you are less likely to be anxious.

> *Philippians 4:6-7 says, "Be anxious for nothing, but in everything by prayer and supplication, with thanksgiving let your requests be made known to God; 7 and the peace of God, which surpasses all understanding, will guard your hearts and minds through Christ Jesus".*

When you are always praying, you find yourself at peace. So, when a situation arises, you don't have to pray specifically for peace. You already have peace. It is a part of your everyday life. You must continue to walk in it. Although situations may occur to disturb your peace, and you may struggle for the moment, you will always bounce back to your place of peace. When my mother passed away, I struggled to find that place of peace in my life. I will not try to pretend that it was easy to reconcile with her leaving. I still struggle from time to time, so when I say peace, I mean I do not allow grief to overtake me. When I feel like I want to lose it, I begin to pray. The Holy Spirit always speaks to my spirit and reminds me of who God is in my life. He reminds me that my mother was a believer and that she is resting in God. He reminds me that I have victory. It is in those times that I find my place of peace.

> *Ephesians 6:12 says, "For we wrestle not against flesh and blood, but against principalities, against powers,*

against the rulers of the darkness of this world, against
spiritual wickedness in high places."

Too often, we spend our time fighting people instead of the reason the person is behaving the way they are. I know this is hard to do, especially when you are being directly attacked by lies, slander, and character assassination. It is natural to want to retaliate and defend yourself. Who wouldn't want to set the record straight and dispel all the rumors against you? How would anyone expect you not to react when someone is standing before being disrespectful and rude? I know my first reaction would be to clap back, making sure they know they are not dealing with a weakling. Believe me, I am certainly not asking you to allow people to ride rough shod over you, but I want you to look at how the enemy can sometimes make you react instead of responding. Often, when we do not use wisdom in recognizing our enemy, we kill the wrong person. We wound someone that doesn't even realize they are just a pawn in the devil's plan and that he is using them to create a disruption. His main goal is to get us distracted.

The enemy is the master manipulator, and he is good at distraction. If he can distract us, he can keep us off our game. When this happens, he can sneak in, cause havoc and confusion, and it seems like he is winning. But if you can simply get your focus right and concentrate on the REAL adversary, you will be able to see him when he comes. If you see him as he comes, you will then know how to address the situation and your results will be The Victory!

Knowing your opponent will help you win every time. You will not waste valuable time fighting a cause that will offer you nothing. When David fought Goliath, it didn't take him much effort to defeat the latter, because he knew his enemy. He recognized that his brothers were not his enemy, though they were talking trash and trying to discourage him. David did not focus on what they had to say about him. I am sure they were taunting him because he was the little brother, and he was only there to deliver their food. How could he possibly be capable of killing a giant, when he had never even been to war?

Had David focused on what they were saying and their feelings about his presence, he probably would have wasted time arguing with them. He would have turned the entire situation into a drama-filled and futile war of words

I believe David first had to conquer the distraction of what his brothers were saying so that he could get to Goliath. This was his main objective. I also believe that because he learned to focus on the enemy and not his brothers, he was prepared when he got to his purpose.

He did not let Goliath's trash-talking distract or frustrate him because he had already dealt with it from his brothers. Often, we lose our concentration because of small things when those things are there to help us stay prepared for a larger battle. It builds our character and teaches us self-control. David had to have self-control when dealing with his brothers and with Goliath.

Practicing self-control in battle is crucial because it makes the difference between life and death, victory and defeat. I remember the times when I did not use self-control and other times when I did, and boy, the outcomes were VASTLY different.

Don't play with YOUR VICTORY

One of the areas I had to learn to apply to recognize my enemy was in my marriage. Can I tell you that was a difficult area to maneuver? The first thing I wanted to do when confronted with a challenge in our marriage was lash out. When I was hurt or offended, I didn't see the enemy. I was not even really looking for the enemy. I saw my husband as enemy number one, period! Of course, having that viewpoint is never good. I messed up every time and things became bigger than they had to be because we were both fighting the wrong enemy. We wasted years of energy and precious time fighting each other instead of ganging up on the real enemy and walking in victory in our marriage.

We have been married for twenty-nine years and we still

must work hard in this area. It is so easy to be distracted by our emotions and the words being said. I must admit there have been times when we look back after a disagreement and could clearly see that it was fueled by the darts of the enemy, and we fell for the trick. We had to regroup and try to do better the next time.

David was successful because he knew why he was fighting, and who he was fighting. Therefore, he knew how to win! When you know who you are fighting, Victory Is Your Only Option.

Victory Notes

Thought Prompters:
Why am I fighting?
Who am I fighting?

_____

_____

_____

_____

_____

_____

_____

_____

_____

_____

_____

_____

_____

_____

_____

_____

_____

KNOW YOUR WEAPON

When I met my husband, he was a security police officer in the Air Force. I knew nothing about what he did. All I knew was he was awfully handsome in his uniform and beret that the security police wore, and it showed off that dimple. Oh, and my Lord, that smile! He had me the first day he came into the Sports Store where I worked, but I couldn't let him know that.

He was a part of the elite gate guard. One thing I remember about him was that when he was on duty, he was authorized to carry a weapon. I would drive through the gate and see him with that weapon on his side. There were other times I saw him, and he would have an M16 across his back. I remember one Thanksgiving he had to work, and we were dating at the time. My mother cooked a big meal, and because she loved him so much, she had me take him some dinner. Well, this shift, he was working in the armory, where all the weapons and ammunition were stored. He sat behind a window where the weapons were, and he issued the weapons to the cops on duty and took them back when they went off duty. In the armory, there were many types of weapons, stacked wall-to-wall. I was lost because I had no idea what any of them were.

After dating for a while, I recall him talking about his weapons training. I didn't quite understand what that meant at first, but he explained that when he became a security police officer, he had to learn about his weapon. They were not just issued a firearm. Before they could fire it, they had to learn how it worked. There was training on how to take the gun apart and reassemble it. They had to learn how to put the safety on and take it off. They had to learn where to put the bullets and how to get them in the chamber. They also had to know the capability of the weapon-the maximum effective range- and the magazine capacity. They had to learn about their weapon before they could ever pull the trigger.

I am afraid that we too often have weapons, and we don't know what they are, much less how to use them. We go to a service, get saved, hear a powerful Word and think we have it – knowing only a verse or two. However, we do not diligently study, so we never learn to correctly explain and use the word of truth. Instead, we shoot weapons with no knowledge and miss the target every time. We have casualties of our misguided, scripturally out-of-context bullets, and we think it's everybody else's fault. The fact is, too often we try to win the battle with weapons we aren't qualified to use. If we want victory, we must learn the basics!

You can't just look the part. You must be willing to do what is necessary to be a master at this. You can't be armed but have no idea of the power of the weapon you carry. Do you understand the responsibility of carrying the weapon?

I believe the reason my husband and others in his squadron had to start by learning about the weapon was so they could see how much power it had. They needed to understand the responsibility they had in carrying this weapon.

To obtain victory, you have to read your Bible more than on Sunday morning when the Pastor reads the scripture from his/her text. The Bible is the manual for the weapons we use, and if you don't read the manual, you won't know how to operate the weapon.

> *Psalms 119:111 says, "Thy word have I hid in mine heart, that I might not sin against thee".*

If you don't read the manual, you won't know the true purpose of the weapon you are using.

> *Proverbs 4:7 says, "Wisdom is the principal thing; therefore, get wisdom: and with all thy getting get understanding".*

You must also know which weapon to use and when. One of the things my husband had to understand is that certain firearms did certain things. Remember I told you that they had to know the capability of the weapon, maximum effective range, and magazine capacity. I tell you, it's the same thing in the spirit! You can't use the same weapon for everything. Ask the disciples in Mark 9. They were trying to cast out a devil to no avail, and they asked Jesus why they couldn't do it. They were trying to use the weapon of speaking, but Jesus tells them in verse 29 that they were using the wrong weapon. He said, "*This kind can come forth by nothing but by prayer and fasting*". In other words, speaking to it won't work in this case. You need the weapon of prayer and fasting. There is an old saying that you can't take a stick to a gunfight. You better know your weapons so you can consider the battle you are in and determine the type of defense you need.

Have you ever seen the movie *Harlem Nights*? I love the scene where the gangsters are standing in the alley firing machine guns, and Arsenio Hall's character shoots a little one-shooter pistol. They finally tell him to put that little gun away because it was ineffective and not appropriate for their fight. That's how we are in the spirit. We are armed but not dangerous because we either aren't using the right weapon or simply don't know how to use the one we have. Spiritual Barney Fife's. You have a weapon, but it's not even loaded. Armed, but not dangerous.

> 2 Timothy 3 "having a form of godliness but denying its power".

You look good. You play the part. You sound good. You are armed, but not dangerous. You are no threat to the kingdom of darkness. How is that possible? You have been given the weapons of prayer, weapons of praise, weapons of worship, weapons of giving, weapons of love, and weapons of tongues, but you won't use them. You won't pray, so you don't have any power. You won't open your mouth, so your weapon of praise is powerless. You are trying to fight the enemy of depression with a little single-shooter revolver (only praising when you come to church and even that, barely). You need an m-60 machine gun kind of praise! An m-60 machine gun is known for its continuous firepower. What does that look like in the spirit?

> David said it in Psalms 34:1, "I will bless the Lord at all times and His praise shall continually be in my mouth".

Once you learn your weapon, you must qualify on your weapon. After the squadron learned about the weapon, they had to learn how to shoot the weapon; not just shoot the weapon, but know how to hit a target. It does no good to aim at a target, fire the weapon, and miss. Two things can happen in this instance. You aim and miss, and what you were intending to hit remains unchanged, or you aim and miss and hit something else. Too often, we think because we come to church and turn around three times, high-five our neighbor four times, and run around the building five times, everything is going to be alright. I need you to know that you must have the right weapon, and you must have the right aim, to hit the target in the kingdom. Let me give you an example.

Galatians 6:7 says, "*Be not deceived; God is not mocked: for whatsoever a man soweth, that shall he also reap*".
The Bible says therefore if I want love, I must sow love. If I want peace, I must sow peace. If I want friends, I must be friendly. If I want money, I must sow money. I can't be stingy and think God is going to bless me. I can dance until I am blue in the face. I can shout until I fall out, but if I haven't put a seed in the ground, it isn't coming up.

2 Corinthians 9:6 says, "*But this I say, He which soweth sparingly shall reap also sparingly; and he which soweth bountifully shall reap also bountifully*".
By understanding the Word...Your weapon... you will be dangerous because nobody will be able to prevent your sowing. When you become proficient with the weapon of prayer, no devil in hell can stop you. The devil will hate to see you get out of bed because you destroy too many of his plans with your m-60, grenade-launching prayers. In other words, when you know your weapon, you can be assured of Victory.

When I recently asked my husband which weapon he qualified on, he proudly told me he was qualified as a sharpshooter on several firearms. This meant no matter which one they gave him, he could hit the target.

You need to be a spiritual sharpshooter who not only knows your weapons and which one to use but is qualified to use them. The Kingdom of God needs spiritual sharpshooters who can hit the target every time and take out the enemy. They understand that the weapons of our warfare are not carnal but are mighty through God. They know what their weapons do...

To the pulling down of strongholds, casting down imaginations and every high thing that exalts itself against the knowledge of Christ, and bringing into captivity every thought to the obedience of Christ. 2 Corinthians 10:4

Are you ready to hit the target in the spirit? Are you ready to be armed and dangerous? This means you have a weapon, you know how to use it, and you know when to use it in the battle. That's the type of person I want to go along with to fight the enemy. That is the type of person that understands Victory Is Their Only Option!

Victory Notes

Thought Prompters:
What weapons are you an expert in using?
Which ones do you need to refresh your skills in using?
Journal a plan for doing so.

_____

_____

_____

_____

_____

_____

_____

_____

_____

_____

_____

_____

_____

_____

_____

THE STRATEGY

No conflict is ever won without a strategy. Winning your battle is going to take strategy; so get yourself together and focus. This is not the time to panic and forget everything you know. Nor is it the time to lose your mind and overreact.

I often tell the agents on my team they must remain calm when something happens with one of the real estate transactions. This is because when you are frazzled and upset, you cannot think. When you cannot think, you cannot figure out what to do next. In other words, you cannot come up with a strategy when your mind is cluttered with too many things.

The attack of the enemy is real, and he is not playing with you.

> *John 10:10 says, "The thief cometh not, but for to steal, and to kill, and to destroy".*

He is not happy just to steal. He will not stop at killing you. His ultimate goal is to destroy you. With an enemy like that, you must stay prayed up. His only focus is to annihilate you. You are playing games and his play is deadly real, literally.

You must continue to seek God's face for strategy and stay focused enough to execute the strategy. How will you know when you are NOT continuing to seek God's face? It looks like knowing the Word but not applying the Word. It looks like knowing the Word, but still speaking death. It looks like knowing the Word but choosing to believe your situation and circumstances over the word.

We receive strategy from the Word. We receive strategy in prayer. We receive strategy in worship. You must keep yourself open to the voice of the Holy Spirit as He speaks strategically to your situation.

You must be in tune with the Holy Spirit during every attack because every attack requires a different strategy to repulse. Often, we try to use old strategies for new incidents. When we do this, it fails because the enemy already knows your strategy. Sometimes, he can anticipate your move because you have not been before God seeking Him for new directions and fresh maneuvers.

> *Proverbs 3:6 says, acknowledge Him in all your ways*
> *and He will direct your path.*

That sounds like a strategy to me. Have you asked the Holy Spirit for advice or direction? The Holy Spirit has not just any strategy, but a winning strategy.

> *Isaiah 55:8(NLT) says, "My thoughts are nothing like*
> *your thoughts, says the Lord, And my ways are far*
> *beyond anything you could imagine".*

Get ready for God to move you outside your box. His directions and instructions may not be orthodox.

Are you willing to allow God to work in your life the way He wants to, even if it doesn't make sense to you? God's "crazy" strategies will produce victory every time! Using the right tactic will yield a winning outcome every time.

Psalms 37:23-24 AMP The steps of a good and righteous man are directed and established by the Lord and He delights in his way (and blesses his path) 24 When he falls, he will not be hurled down, because the Lord is the One who holds his hand and sustains him.

Following God's direction will lead you to victory and even if you fall, you will not be destroyed. There are benefits to following God's strategy. Another word for this is **direction**.

What happens when we follow His direction?

 He Directs:

This means to control the operations of; manage or govern.

- *Proverbs 3:6 In all thy ways acknowledge him, and he shall direct thy paths.*
- *Psalms 5:8 lead me in the right path, o Lord, or my enemies will conquer me. Make your way plain for me to follow.*
- *Psalms 119:105 Your word is a lamp to guide my feet and a light for my path.*
- *Psalms 32:8 The Lord says, "I will guide you along the best pathway for your life. I will advise you and watch over you".*
- *Psalms 119:133 Guide my steps by your word, so I will not be overcome by evil.*

When you follow His direction, you never have to worry about whether His info is updated.

 **He Blesses:**

You need to follow his direction because blessings are there. God knows where the blessings are; so if you follow Him, He will lead you to what He has already blessed. Stop trying to figure it out for yourself, try to go your own way, and follow His direction. Stop trying to get God to bless what you are doing and do what God has already blessed.

> Deuteronomy 28:1-6 (AMP) "Now it shall be, if you diligently listen to and obey the voice of the Lord your God, being careful to do all of His commandments which I am commanding you today, the Lord your God will set you high above all the nations of the earth. ² All these blessings will come upon you and overtake you if you pay attention to the voice of the Lord your God. "You will be blessed in the city, and you will be blessed in the field". ⁴ "The offspring of your body and the produce of your ground and the offspring of your animals, the offspring of your herd and the young of your flock will be blessed". ⁵ "Your basket and your kneading bowl will be blessed". ⁶ "You will be blessed when you come in and you will be blessed when you go out".

 He Sustains:

As long as you walk with God, you don't have to worry about falling or failing because he will support and sustain you. God will take care of you. He may have to reroute you because you missed a turn, but don't worry. He will sustain you. He will ensure that you get back on track.

> Psalms 55:22 Cast your burden on the Lord [release it] and He will sustain and uphold you; He will never allow the righteous to be shaken (slip, fall, fail).

He gives you strength for the journey.

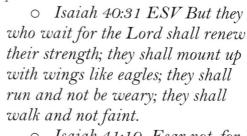

FIND STRATEGY IN *Prayer*

- o *Isaiah 40:29 He gives strength to the weary, and to him who has no might, He increases power.*
- o *Isaiah 40:31 ESV But they who wait for the Lord shall renew their strength; they shall mount up with wings like eagles; they shall run and not be weary; they shall walk and not faint.*
- o *Isaiah 41:10 Fear not, for I am with you; be not dismayed, for I am your God; I will strengthen you, I will help you, I will uphold you with my righteous right hand.*
- o *2 Corinthians 12:9 But he said to me, "My grace is sufficient for you, for my power is made perfect in weakness." Therefore, I will boast all the more gladly of my weaknesses, so that the power of Christ may rest upon me.*
- o *Isaiah 26:3 ESV You keep him in perfect peace whose mind is stayed on you because he trusts in you.*

Don't go your own way. Stop trying to take shortcuts. Follow His direction. With God's plan, you better believe Victory Is Your Only Option!

Victory Notes

Thought Prompters:
What is God's strategy for my Life?
How can I be more in tune with His direction?

VICTORY OVER ME

Numbers 13:33 says, "And there we saw the giants, the sons of Anak which come of the giants and we were in our own sight a. grasshoppers, and so we were in their sight."

In this text, the spies were sent to look at the land that had been promised to them. They were sent to look at what they could have, but all they could see was what was blocking them from getting it. When I read this passage, I see a few things. First, God instructs Moses to send out a man from every tribe to spy out the land that was already theirs. He wanted a report about what was there. It may not look like it right now, but God has already given you victory. The truth is, you will go through some things and there will always be situations and circumstances.

What you are experiencing is true and real. The hurt you feel is real. The disappointment you face is real. The bills are real. The doctor's report is real. I do not want you to think that because you are a believer, nothing is ever going to happen. I simply want you to look at where you are and what is going on, so you are aware, but it does not change the fact you are victorious. It may seem like a lot i going on, but the promise belongs to you. Look at it, but do not dwell on it. Do not allow what you are going through to define your victory.

Don't waste time talking about the obstacles you see before you but spend time talking about what is promised to you. Imagine yourself accessing all that God has in store for you.

Additionally, I noticed that although they saw some challenges in the Promised Land, there were also some good things.

> *Numbers 13:23 says, "And they came unto the brook Eshcol, and cut down from thence a branch with one cluster of grapes, and they bare it between two upon a staff; and they brought of the pomegranates and of the fig."*

God will bless you in the middle of what you are going through! Notice in the text that the grapes were so big, it took two of them to carry the clusters. You need to get ready because right in the middle of God showing you the promise and your possessing your promise, there are some big blessings. They got a chance to taste what was promised to them. God will allow you to experience small victories along the way that will encourage you when you have to face bigger challenges.

Let's delve a little deeper and look at the report the ten spies came back with, *versus* the one the two came back with. The ten were already defeated–not by any outside opinion, but by their own. They saw themselves defeated before they even started. Sometimes, the biggest enemy you will ever confront is YOU. You can stop yourself faster than any outside force ever can. You can convince yourself that you won't be able to win. You can talk yourself out of trying something new or pursuing your dreams, before even they can form. The bondage of self-doubt and lack of self-grace can render you paralyzed in your pursuit of being what God wants you to be.

The worst thing you can do is to compare yourself to what you see. The spies said they saw themselves as grasshoppers. Their opinion of themselves could not beat what was standing in front of them because of its size. Have you ever felt that way? Have you felt what you were facing was too big and too overwhelming for you to deal with, let alone actually triumph over? The spies didn't know they were already victorious, and the land already belonged to them. God just wanted them to go see where he was taking them. The Bible says as a man thinks in his heart, so he is. If you see yourself as a loser or defeated, you will behave that way. You will make losing decisions; accept a defeated life and will allow others to treat you in ways you do not deserve. A distorted perspective of yourself can cause you to lose the battle before you even begin.

I often watch athletes before a game. I notice they are focused, and they sometimes have headphones on, listening to music. My son, who played football, says they do this to get their mind right. They usually listen to music that encourages them about who they are and what they can achieve on the field so that when they come out, they are ready to win. They listen to songs that pump them up about winning. They must see themselves as champions and conquering the enemy. You must do the same. See yourself as a winner. See yourself making the right plays in life. See yourself the way God sees you–Victorious!

The way you see yourself is the way other people will see you. The spies said they saw themselves as grasshoppers, and so did the enemy. If you see yourself defeated, other people will treat you as such. You need to change your perspective so that those around you will change their perspective of you. Don't talk about yourself in a negative light, or admit to a lack of ability to win. The way you see yourself will also reflect in the words you use for self-talk.

Let's try an experiment. You can do this now if you're able to. Go to the mirror, stand there, and talk to yourself. Encourage yourself. Love yourself. Tell yourself that you are "fearfully and wonderfully made". Proclaim that you are a royal priesthood, the apple of God's eye. Usually, we tell ourselves all kinds of defeatist things...I'm too fat...I am not smart enough...I am not pretty enough...I will never make it through this...., and so on.

The truth of the matter is I had to live this chapter myself. When my mother passed away, I was in the middle of writing this book. Her death was a gut punch that took the breath out of me. I felt I had lost my confidence because my biggest cheerleader was no longer with me. Yes, I had my husband, my dad, my sisters, my children, and others who loved me, but her voice was the one I had heard the loudest and the longest all my life.

I was fighting depression, lack of confidence, doubt and so much more. The enemy said things to me like "no one wants to read your book," "you are not a writer and people are going to critique you," "They will laugh at what you wrote," "It won't help anyone". Now I knew all this was a lie, but I allowed it to stay in my spirit too long and before I knew it, I started to believe it. I was like the spies and saw myself as a grasshopper in my own eyes.

It was easy to encourage others and tell them how powerful they were. I had been able to get other women FIRED UP, but I felt I barely had a spark. I allowed the enemy's lies to manifest as truth in my mind and I was stuck. I felt cornered and wasn't using my weapons. I was my own enemy. It took time for prayer and talking with someone to help me overcome my feelings of self-doubt and lack of confidence.

I am challenging you to see yourself differently and triumph over <u>yourself</u>. Don't be your own biggest obstacle. Get out of your own way! The enemy didn't have to stop the spies. They decided about themselves based on their current situation. Often, people do the same thing. They base their outcome and their victory on what is before them instead of the success they already have.

The saying is, stop looking at the glass as half empty and see it as half full. That is the mindset of a victorious person. Even though things may appear not to be working out, the victorious person looks for the good and focuses on that. You must find a reason to rejoice. I am not saying you rejoice for everything, but as the scripture says, rejoice **in** everything. When you have a victorious mindset, you can rejoice. Don't miss your moment of victory!

Don't Miss Your Moment

Let's look at *John 5:1-5* to see how a single moment can change your life.

> *After this, there was a feast of the Jews, and Jesus went up to Jerusalem. 2 Now there is in Jerusalem by the Sheep Gate a pool, in Aramaic called Bethesda, which has five roofed colonnades. 3 In these lay a multitude of invalids—blind, lame, and paralyzed. 5 One man was there who had been an invalid for thirty-eight years*
> *One moment of getting the victory over you and your thinking can change your life.*

This is the story at the pool of Bethesda, as the man waits for someone to put him in the pool when it was stirred once a year. The custom was that whoever got to the pool first, would be healed. The man was so concerned about his circumstances and where he was that he almost missed his moment of victory over his sickness. He didn't realize that Jesus was not confined to the customs, and He was not confined to the stirring of the pool. At that moment, he had to get over himself.

 **The Right Moment Can Change Your Life**

It doesn't matter how long you have been waiting. Don't miss your moment. This man had been suffering for thirty-eight years. That was a long time. He had been unable to move, to produce. The only thing he saw from day to day was the desperation of his situation and the circumstances of so many others like him. He was surrounded by people hurting as he did, all wanting the same thing he did. They were all waiting for the angel to come and stir the water, but on this day, this man received his victory because of one moment with Jesus. No matter how long you have been in the situation you are in, no matter how many times you have had to watch others get their blessing, no matter for how long you have been waiting for that one moment, just one moment, the right encounter with God can change your life.

Your Moment Will Be Out Of the Norm

You have been looking for God to move one way. Don't expect Him to move the way you have seen Him move in the past. Don't limit God to the way He moved for someone else. Don't look for the way everyone told you it was supposed to be. God is looking for people who are not going to put Him in a box. Look at it like the song goes, any way you bless me, Lord, I'll be satisfied. Sometimes, the moment is not going to come conventionally. Don't miss your moment because you can't see God doing something different.

> Isaiah 43:19 says, "For I am about to do something new. See, I have already begun! Do you not see it? I will make a pathway through the wilderness. I will create rivers in the dry wasteland".

The man's response to Jesus was to tell Him how things worked around there. When Jesus asked him if he wanted to be healed, he said, *"I can't because I don't have anyone to put me in the pool. Somebody always gets there first".*

Your moment may not be in the movement. I know that's the way it has been done, but that isn't your moment. It worked for everybody else, but it is not what God has for you. When the man finished telling Jesus why he couldn't get healed, Jesus disregarded everything he said and simply responded with, *"Stand up, take up your bed and walk"*. In other words, you can't always depend on someone else, and you can't always blame somebody else, even if no one else helps.

You Have to Participate in Your Moment

Stop waiting on someone else to get you to your moment. This move, this moment in your life, will require you to do what you have to. You must want it badly enough to go for it. This man had been this way for 38 years and now Jesus says stand up. How did this happen? The man got up on a word and the word spoke to what was already in him. It didn't look like he had the strength. I am sure everyone around him, including the man, would have never thought he could do it. But when a word from God connects to your spirit, you can do things you never knew you could. Jesus already knew his potential. Now it was up to the man to trust Jesus.

Stop arguing with God about what He is telling you to do. If He is telling you to do it, it is because He knows what He put inside you. He just needs you to move at His word. Your response needs to be like that of Mary in *Luke 1:38*, *"Be it unto me according to your word"*. You must get the victory over yourself. You need to declare, "I will participate with God's word for my moment". You don't have to have all the answers. Just move when God says so and do what He tells you to. The man got up and picked up his bed as Jesus told him to. He didn't tell him what to do with the bed. He didn't ask Jesus 50 million questions… So….should I stand up fast or slow? Should I roll over first, then get up on my knees and push my way up? Should I fold the bed in a square or rectangle???

Sometimes you miss your moment because you ask too many questions and talk yourself right out of it. What is God telling you? What instructions has He given you? Don't let where you are, and who you are surrounded by, make you miss your moment. One moment of hearing the right word and making the decision to respond to that word can make a difference to whether you stay where you are, or whether you will be healed and walk into your VICTORY. Stop looking for your moment in conventional ways. Be ready to think out of the box. Be willing to let God move in your life however He wants to. Don't get stuck with a one-track mind but be ready to flow with the Spirit. Be ready to participate in your moment. It's time for you to start moving. It's time for your faith to be stretched. It's time to stop talking about it and start going for it. If no one else moves, you must be ready to move.

The text says, Jesus saw the man and how long he had been that way. I want you to know that God sees you. He knows how long you have been that way, but don't get comfortable. Be ready to participate in your moment. Be ready to move when He tells you to. Be ready to stand up. Be ready to take up your mat. Be ready to walk. I know this is not proper English but, "Whatchu gone do"? Will your reply be, "I'm ready for my moment"? Will you get the victory over yourself and walk out the promises of God in your life? My moment may not look like your moment, but that's ok. DON'T MISS YOUR MOMENT by being your own worst enemy. You have to say, I don't care what I'm surrounded by. I'm coming out of this thing. I am waiting for my moment, and when it arrives, I will be ready! I will no longer stop ME from walking to my victory.

Victory Notes

Thought Prompters:
What have I stopped myself from doing?
What moments have I missed that Jesus is now trying to
move on my behalf in?

_____

_____

_____

_____

_____

_____

_____

_____

_____

_____

_____

_____

_____

_____

_____

_____

YOU ARE VICTORIOUS!

VICTORY is your only option, so lift your heads oh ye gates! and be ye lifted up you everlasting doors! Lift your head, square your shoulders, and let the enemy know that you are not defeated, and you will not live a life of defeat. Accept the victory Christ gave you and walk in it. Do not allow feelings of inadequacy to make you shrink from what God has already given you. You have the victory. All you must do is show up.

> *Psalms 34:19 declares, "Many are the afflictions of the righteous, but the Lord delivers them out of them all".*

I own a property management company and there was a time I had to go to court for an eviction. I normally do not attend those proceedings, but I went this time to assist the new property manager because this was her first time. When we got to the court, we were expecting the tenant to be there because when we filed the eviction papers, the tenant replied to the court and wanted to challenge the eviction. Remember I told you earlier that the enemy is not going to allow you to just walk into your victory. He will challenge you. He will try to intimidate you. So, we prepared for court. We gathered information from the files specific to the property, the tenant's payment history, and other correspondence (sounds like searching out the scriptures to me). In other words, we did not go in blindly but prepared for the battle. We then sat down and discussed our strategy, such as who was going to say what. We rehearsed not what the tenant had done, but our documents with his payment history, etc.

> SIDENOTE: *When you go into battle, stop talking about what the enemy has and focus on what you have, which is the truth. See, the records we had did not lie.*

We arrived at court and waited for the tenant, to start. The judge comes in and calls the court to order and began calling the cases. When he got to our case, he called my company and we responded "HERE". The assistant then calls the tenant's name and, lo and behold, the tenant did not respond. The judge gave everyone in the room ten minutes to try to work things out amongst themselves. After ten minutes, they call the roll again and moved up the cases that had only one party present. Our case moved to the top of the list.

Somebody reading this needs to know that God is not only about to give you the victory, but He is about to move you to another level. You are about to "level up". Our case was called, and we stood before the judge, presented our evidence of non-payment and outstanding rent, and the judge granted us the Writ of Possession. At that point, I told the judge that not only did the tenant fail to pay, but as of the night before our hearing date, we checked the house and discovered that the tenant had moved out of the house and disconnected the power and water. The judge then granted us not only the writ of possession, which gives the tenant seven days to vacate, but also immediate possession. The entire process took a mere three minutes. The judge said because we showed up, we automatically won. And not only did we win, but we also received immediate possession. As I was walking out of the courtroom, he told me, 'All you had to do was show up'.

Regardless of what people try to say about you and what the enemy is trying to use to discourage you, just show up! Show up with your praise. Show up with your hands lifted in victory. Show up declaring God's Word.

Your victory is inevitable. Why? Because Jesus said so. He said he has already overcome the world. In other words, He has already won your victory. God has already made the way; so, stop making excuses and walk in it. Take all other options off the table. YOU ARE VICTORIOUS!

Victory Notes

Thought Prompters:
Write positive affirmations to yourself

_____

_____

_____

_____

_____

_____

_____

_____

_____

_____

_____

_____

_____

_____

_____

_____

_____

TO CONNECT WITH THE AUTHOR

Co-Pastor Freida McCullough is a powerful speaker and ignitor of the purpose and potential that lies dormant in others. As a minister, mentor to women, motivational speaker, corporate leadership trainer, and savvy businesswoman, she empowers and equips others to passionately pursue being what God created them to be.

FOR MORE INFORMATION OR TO **CONNECT** WITH US FOR BOOKING, SPEAKING, OR MORE – GO TO WWW.FREIDASPEAKS.COM AND CHECK OUT OUR STORE FOR *VICTORY...YOUR ONLY OPTION* MERCH AND MORE!

JOIN OUR MAILING LIST! EMAIL CONNECT@FMMINISTRIES.COM

LET US KNOW WHAT YOU THINK ABOUT THE BOOK! EMAIL CONNECT@FMMINISTRIES.COM OR CONNECT ON THE WEBSITE. **COMING SOON**! AUDIOBOOK AND FACILITATOR GUIDE FOR LIFE GROUPS

FOLLOW ON SOCIAL MEDIA:
FACEBOOK: @FREIDASPEAKS
INSTAGRAM: @FREIDA.SPEAKS
YOUTUBE: @FREIDA MCCULLOUGH

Made in the USA
Columbia, SC
22 December 2021

50855521R00050